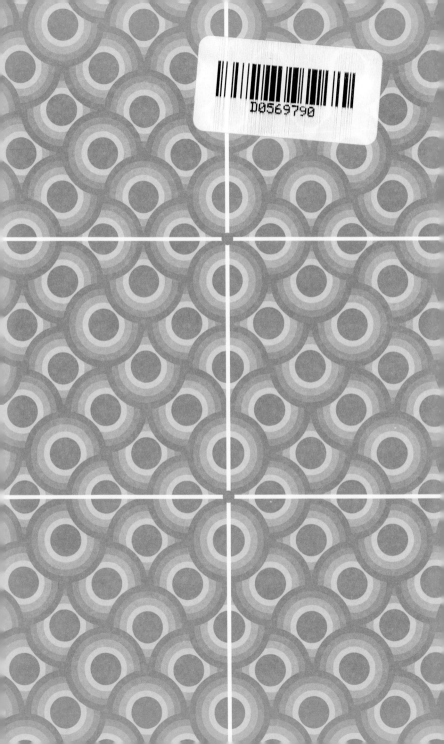

D0569790

The Very Embarrassing Book of Dad Jokes

First published in the United Kingdom in 2012 by
Portico
43 Great Ormond Street
London
WC1N 3HZ

An imprint of Pavilion Books Company Limited

ISBN 978-1-907554-53-7

A CIP catalogue record for this book is available from the
British Library.

22

Printed and bound by CPI Group (UK) Ltd, Croydon, CR0 4YY

This book can be ordered direct from the publisher at
www.pavilionbooks.com

The Very Embarrassing Book of Dad Jokes

Ian Allen

PORTICO

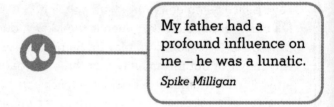

My father had a profound influence on me – he was a lunatic.

Spike Milligan

Hello!

Let's get one thing straight from the start. Dads' jokes aren't meant to be funny. The perfect dad joke should generate groans not guffaws, dewy-eyed nostalgia rather than cries of 'That's a new one!' and pitying glances not affectionate smiles.

But although dads love telling jokes, lots of them have difficulty remembering them – their heads are too full of important stuff like 'when is the M.O.T. due' and 'who do Crewe Alexandra play on Saturday' – which is why they trot out the same two or three old gags time after time after time. This book now gives you 1,000 or so new old jokes to trot out time after time; just memorising three every morning while on the toilet will allow you to annoy your kids with a year's supply of he-he-seeking missiles.

If I give you an example of a joke that failed to make the cut, you'll get some idea of the comedic nirvana that awaits you in the rest of the book:

Teacher: Mr Smith, I think you should buy Jimmy an encyclopedia.

Dad: Rubbish, he can walk to school just like I had to.

You get the picture!

This joke book is the result of literally days of research into Christmas crackers, the backs of cereal packets and dog-eared copies of the *Dandy*. (I even borrowed a library book containing Ancient Greek 'jokes', and all I can say is that it proves the old ones most definitely aren't the best.) If I had only known how handy they would have been, I would have kept all my lolly sticks with jokes on from the 1970s, instead of letting my mum throw them away last year.

Most of the jokes in these pages were either dredged up from the dusty reaches of my memory or else, when I rediscovered them in print or online, gave me that warm feeling you get when you meet an old friend you had quite forgotten about. A few, though, were new to me, and therefore might not be thought old enough to merit inclusion in a classic dads' joke book. But I think they all meet the dad joke criteria – if you tell them often enough and badly enough, you can remove any hint of humour from even the funniest of them.

Never forget, dads, your children are wonderful; just remember what philosopher John Locke said:

Children are travellers newly arrived in a strange country of which they know nothing.

And that in a nutshell is why dads who tell jokes have large families – because the single greatest thing about being a dad is that every time you have another kid you get to tell all your jokes for the first time ... again!

And if you only happen to have one or two kids, there's no need to worry. A wise man once pointed out that no one should be ashamed of telling a joke more than once as, after all, no one complains when their favourite piece of music is played repeatedly – so remember it's important to get your money's worth!

Finally, a health warning: attempting to read more than 50 or 60 jokes as bad as these in one sitting could have serious long-term health consequences. For your own sake stop reading after a dozen or so and go for a nice long walk, mow the lawn or sit down in the front of the telly with a cold beer. You'll feel better. And so will the family.

Enjoy!

Why did the orange stop halfway up the hill?
He ran out of juice.

What's the richest country in the world?
Ireland, because its capital is always Dublin.

What's worse than finding a worm in your apple?
Finding half a worm.

William Shakespeare went into a pub.
The barman took one look at him and said,
'You're bard!'

First man: I'm going to see the doctor because
I don't like the look of my wife.
Second man: I'll come with you, I can't stand the
sight of mine.

First man: How many people work in your office?
Second man: About half of them.

I once had a dog with no legs called Woodbine.
Every day I'd take him out for a drag.

What do you call a
sheep with no legs?

A cloud.

First man: I once knew a man with a wooden leg called Smith.
Second man: Really, what was his other leg called?

Son: What are you getting Mum for her birthday?
Dad: A new bag and belt … the hoover hasn't been working very well lately.

What's brown, steams and comes out of cows backwards?
The Isle of Wight ferry.

What do you get if you drop a piano down a coal shaft?
A flat minor.

How does an intruder get into your house?

In t'ru der window.

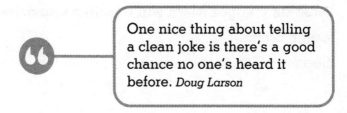

One nice thing about telling a clean joke is there's a good chance no one's heard it before. *Doug Larson*

What do you call a man with a seagull on his head?
Cliff.

What do you call a man with a piece of grass and a seagull on his head?
Heathcliff.

What's yellow and dangerous?
Shark-infested custard.

Did you hear about the man who drowned in a bowl of muesli?
He was pulled under by a strong currant.

What do you get when you run over a sparrow with a lawnmower?
Shredded Tweet.

What's yellow and swings through the jungle smelling of almonds?
Tarzipan.

Why do milking stools only have three legs?
Because the cow has the udder.

How does an elephant get down from a tree?
He sits on a leaf and waits until autumn.

DAD STAT

67% of dads admit to trying to pass off successful jokes as their own, when really they just heard them on the TV or stumbled across them on the Internet.

Patient: Doctor, I feel like a snooker ball.
Doctor: Get to the end of the queue!

Patient: Doctor, I keep forgetting everything.
Doctor: How long has this been going on?
Patient: How long has what been going on?

Where did Napoleon keep his armies?
Up his sleevies.

Where are the Andes?
At the end of your armies.

Why did the banana go to the doctors'?
Because he wasn't peeling very well.

First man: Tell me, do you file your nails?
Second man: No, I just cut them off and throw them away.

How do you get into a house with no doors and no windows?
Keep running round it until you're all in.

First man: I had a wooden car once – wooden doors, wooden wheels, even a wooden engine.
Second man: Really, how was it?
First man: It wooden go.

How do you tell if a worm is a boy worm or a girl worm?
Tell it a joke – if he laughs it's a boy, and if she laughs it's a girl.

Boy: Dad, there's a man at the door with a bill.

Dad: Don't be daft, son, it must be a duck with a hat on.

What do you call a man with a plank on his head?

Edward.

What do you call a man with three planks on his head?

Edward Woodward.

What do you call a man with something brown and sticky on his head?

Jedward.

What's the difference between a jeweller and a prison warden?
One sells watches and the other watches cells.

Dad: What's the difference between an elephant and a postbox?
Son: I don't know.
Dad: I'd better not give you my letters to post, then.

Who's the quickest draw on the seabed?
Billy the Squid.

What lies on the seabed and shivers?
A nervous wreck.

Stupid answers kids give to questions

What is a glacier? Someone who mends broken windows.

Where does a kangeroo keep her baby? In her porch.

What is a vacuum? A large empty place where the Pope lives.

What did Moses bring down from Mount Sinai? The tabloids.

What did Socrates die of? An overdose of wedlock.

What's grey, has four legs
and a trunk?
A mouse going on holiday.

What's black and shoots out of the ground shouting 'Knickers!'
Crude oil.

What's orange and travels at 100mph?
A turbo-charged carrot.

What's big, black, bounces and goes ding-dong?
A rubber cathedral.

Why shouldn't you play cards in the jungle?
There are too many cheetahs.

How do you make toast in the jungle?
Pop your bread under a g'rilla.

What's green and goes up and down?
A gooseberry in a lift.

What's huge, pink and wobbles?
An inside-out elephant.

What's black and shoots out of the ground shouting 'Underwear!'
Refined oil.

What's big, red and eats rocks?
A big, red rock-eater.

19

A man went into a chip shop and asked for fish and chips twice.

The man behind the counter said, 'I heard you the first time.'

Patient: Doctor, can you give me anything for wind?
Doctor: Have you tried a kite?

What do you call a man with a rug on his head?

Matt.

Why don't polar bears eat penguins?
They can't get the wrappers off.

Two men walked into a bar.
You'd have thought one of them would have seen it.

Why do bakers work so hard?
Because they knead the dough.

Two fish were swimming in a lake when one swam straight into a concrete wall.

'Dam,' he said.

Son: Dad, why haven't you spoken to Mum this week at all?

Dad: Well, son, I don't like to interrupt her.

What's worse than a giraffe with a sore throat?

An elephant with a nose bleed.

Patient: Doctor, my hair is falling out, can you give me something to keep it in?

Doctor: Ask at reception, they'll give you a box.

Why can't you find any aspirin in the jungle?

Because the parrots eat 'em all.

Polar bear cub: Dad, are you sure I'm a polar bear?

Dad polar bear: Of course, son. I'm a polar bear, your mum's a polar bear, all your family are polar bears. Why do you ask?

Cub: Because I'm flipping freezing.

What's the scariest thing in the ocean?

A terror-pin.

What's the difference between a buffalo and a bison?

You can't wash your hands in a buffalo.

What do you get if you cross the Atlantic with the Titanic?

Just over halfway.

What do you get if you cross a sheep with a kangeroo?

A woolly jumper.

What do you get if you cross a sheep with a kangeroo and a zebra?

A stripy woolly jumper.

What do you get if you cross a kangeroo with an elephant?
Great big holes all over Australia.

A man went to the doctors' with custard in one ear and jelly in the other.
The doctor said, 'What's the matter with you?'
The man replied, 'You'll have to speak up, I'm a trifle deaf.'

What do you call a deer with no eyes?
No idea.

What do you call a deer with no eyes that doesn't move?
Still no idea.

What's the difference between a duck?

One of its legs is both the same.

> **What do you call a fish with no eyes?**
>
> Fsh.

Old lady in chip shop: A small bag of chips, please.
Assistant: Would you like some salt and vinegar?
Old lady: Ooh, I don't know. Is it free?
Assistant: Yes, completely free!
Old lady: In that case I'll have two packets of salt and a bottle of vinegar.

Doctor: You appear to have a steering wheel attached to your groin.
Patient: I know, and it's driving me nuts!

Patient: Doctor, I keep thinking I'm a dog.
Doctor: How long has this been going on?
Patient: Ever since I was a puppy.

What do you get if you cross a bee with a lizard?
A blizzard.

Diner: Waiter, these eggs are off.
Waiter: Don't blame me, sir, I only laid the table.

Diner: Waiter, there's a fly in my soup.
Waiter: Don't worry, sir, the spider on your roll will get him.

Patient: Doctor, I feel like I'm a pair of curtains.
Doctor: Pull yourself together!

Did you hear about the mathematician who got a rubber stuck up his nose?
He worked it out with a pencil.

What has twenty legs and flies?
Ten pairs of trousers.

What else has twenty legs and flies?

Five dead horses.

Two goldfish were in a tank.

One says, 'Do you know how to drive this thing?'

Two budgies were standing on a perch.

One says, 'Can you smell fish?'

Patient: Doctor, I'm having trouble sleeping.

Doctor: Lie right on the edge of your bed and you'll soon drop off.

Passenger: Does this bus stop at the end of the pier?

Driver: I hope so, mate!

Dad: When your grandad was in the army he saved the whole regiment.

Son: What did he do?

Dad: He shot the cook.

> **A large hole has appeared in the High Street.**
>
> Council workers are looking into it.

Dad: You promised me you'd make 100 per cent effort at school this week.

Son: I did! Monday 35 per cent, Tuesday 25, 15 on Wednesday and Thursday and 10 on Friday.

Why did the hedgehog cross the road?

To see his flatmate.

Customer: Your hands are filthy!

Hairdresser: It's not my fault. No one's been in for a shampoo yet this morning.

Dad: Are you enjoying the donkey ride, son?
Son: I can't work out how something stuffed full of hay can be so hard!

Teacher: Did you have a nice holiday, Jimmy?
Jimmy: Yes, we went on the beach and Dad buried us in the sand and then we buried Dad in the sand. Mum says we can go back next year and dig him up.

An English cat called One-Two-Three challenged a French cat called Un-Deux-Trois to a race across the English Channel. Which one won?
One-Two-Three won, because the Un-Deux-Trois cat sank.

How did the tap-dancer hurt himself?
He fell in the sink.

How did the Morris dancer hurt himself?
He fell through the windscreen.

The Three Bears returned from their morning walk.
'Someone's been eating my porridge,' said
Daddy Bear.
**'Someone's been eating my porridge,' said
Mummy Bear.**
'Never mind the porridge,' said Baby Bear,
'someone's pinched the X-Box.'

Waiter: And how did you find your steak, sir?
Diner: I just moved a chip and there it was.

Diner: I'd like an elephant sandwich, please.
Waiter: I'm sorry, sir, we've just run out of bread.

Who's the most wanted man in the ocean?
Al Caprawn.

First hippy: Turn the radio on, man.
Second hippy: Hey, radio, I love you ...

Who's the second-most wanted man in the ocean?

Jack the Kipper.

Two men were sitting on the end of a pier when one screamed and shouted, 'A shark just bit off my leg!'

'Which one?'

'I don't know, all sharks look the same to me.'

What's green and pear-shaped?

A pear.

What's blue and square?

An orange in disguise.

Son: Dad, a pigeon just pooed on me.

Dad: Go and get a bit of toilet paper.

Son: Don't be daft, Dad, he'll be miles away by now.

First man: Who was that lady I seen you with last night?

Second man: You mean, 'I saw'.

First man: OK, who was that eyesore I seen you with last night?

What's the fastest thing in the river?
A motorpike and side-carp.

What do sea monsters eat for dinner?
Fish and ships.

First man: My neighbour's dogs are keeping me up all night with their barking.
Second man: You ought to buy the dog off him. Then it'll be him that can't sleep.

Mum: Your dad reminds me of the sea.
Daughter: Oh, you mean wild, restless and romantic?
Mum: No, he just makes me sick.

Son: Mum, come quick, Dad's up to his ankles in wet concrete.
Mum: Typical. But there's no rush, son.
Son: Yes there is, he fell in head-first.

How many ears does Captain Kirk have?

Three: a left ear, a right ear, and a final front ear.

Teacher: If Shakespeare were alive today, what would he be famous for?

Pupil: Being over 400 years old, sir.

Why did the cross-eyed teacher get the sack?
He couldn't control his pupils.

What's the difference between a torn flag and a bent sixpence?
One's a tattered banner and the other's a battered tanner.

What goes snap, crackle?
Two Rice Krispies.

Why have elephants got big ears?
Because Noddy wouldn't pay the ransom.

What do you call a man with a bag of compost on his head?
Pete.

Optician: Have your eyes been checked before?
Man: No, they've always been blue.

Why did the florist sell his shop?
He could see there was no fuchsia in it.

Passenger: Why has the train stopped?

Guard: We've hit a cow, madam.

Passenger: Oh dear, was it on the track?

Guard: No, we had to chase it over a field.

What has two humps and is found at the South Pole?

A very confused camel.

Why did the sailor grab a bar of soap when his ship sank?

To wash himself ashore.

What's a cow's favourite cereal?

Moo-sli.

What's a cat's favourite cereal?

Mice Krispies.

What is bought by the metre and worn by the foot?
A carpet.

What did the ghost teacher say to her class?
Watch the board and I'll go through it again.

What do you call someone with a spade on his head?
Doug.

What do you call someone without a spade on his head?
Douglas.

What has four eyes and one mouth?
The Mississippi.

Where did the hairdresser meet the snooker player?
At a barbecue.

What's the best-dressed country in the world?
Tie-land.

What's an astronaut's favourite time?
12.57 (Three to one!)

Child: Mum, what happens when a car gets too old and clapped-out to work properly?
Mum: Someone sells it to Dad.

A man went into the doctors' with a frog on his head.
The doctor said, 'Good grief, how long have you had that there?'
And the frog said, 'Well, it all started as a boil on my bottom.'

**Man at railway station: I'd like a return
ticket, please.**

Cashier: Certainly, sir, where to?

Man: Back here, of course.

**Dad: I'm thinking of buying a pig and keeping it
in your room.**

Teenager: But what about the smell?

Dad: The pig will just have to get used to it.

How do you burn an idiot on the ear?

Ring him up while he's ironing.

Waiter: Would you like your pizza cut into four pieces or six?

Man: Just four, please, I couldn't manage six slices.

Doctor: I've had your tests back and there's some good news and some bad news. The good news is you've only got 24 hours to live.

Patient: What's the bad news?

Doctor: I should have told you yesterday.

Doctor: I'm afraid to tell you you're suffering from halitosis.

Patient: Well, I'd like a second opinion.

Doctor: OK, you're ugly as well.

Why did the King of Norway wear purple braces?
To keep his trousers up.

Which king of England wore the biggest shoes?
The one with the biggest feet.

Teacher: You should have been here at nine o'clock.

Pupil: Why, what happened?

What do you get if you cross a mouse with an elephant?
Great big holes in your skirting board.

What do you get when you cross a gorilla with a parrot?
I don't know, but when it talks, you listen!

The police arrested two men, one for drinking battery acid, one for eating fireworks.
They charged one and let the other one off.

How do elephants hide in the jungle?
They paint their toenails red and hide in cherry trees.

What's the loudest sound in the jungle?
Giraffes eating cherries.

Teacher: If I have three apples in one hand and four apples in the other hand, what do I have?
Pupil: Flippin' big hands, miss.

What do you call a septic cat?
Puss.

Why was the useless goalkeeper called Dracula?
Because he was afraid of crosses.

Why was the timid defender called Cinderella?
He kept running away from the ball.

What do you call
a man with a kilt
on his head?

Scott.

What do you
call a man with
a nappy on his
head?

Terry.

How do you flatten a ghost?
With a spirit level.

What's the best way to kill a circus?
Go straight for the juggler.

> Did you hear about the dentist who became a brain surgeon?
>
> His drill slipped.

Teacher: What do you want to be when you grow up?

Pupil: I'm going to follow in my father's footsteps and be a detective.

Teacher: I didn't know your father was a policeman.

Pupil: He isn't, he's a burglar.

Did you hear about the man who ran a successful flea circus?

He started it from scratch.

Son: I've got a part in the school play, playing a man who's been married for twenty years.

Dad: Well, do a good job and maybe next time you'll get a speaking part.

How did the baker get an electric shock?
He stood on a bun and a currant ran up his leg.

Why couldn't the archaelogist get promoted?
Because his career was in ruins.

Pupil: Sir, should I be punished for something I haven't done?
Teacher: No, certainly not.
Pupil: Great, I haven't done my homework.

**What training do you need
to be a litter collector?**

None, you just pick it up as you go along.

Did you hear about the lonely man who bought a book from a charity shop called How to Hug?
When he got home he discovered it was volume 12 of the encyclopedia.

Why did the man keep his budgie in a goldfish bowl?
Because the water wouldn't stay in the cage.

Son: What's your opinion of this programme, Dad?
Dad: It makes no sense at all.
Son: I know, but let's hear it anyway.

Teacher: What do you know about Camelot?
Pupil: Is it a parking area in the desert, sir?

A dog walked into a wild west saloon with one leg in a sling. He went up to the bar and said, 'I'm looking for the man that shot my paw.'

What's a bachelor?

Someone who never Mrs anyone.

Patient: Doctor, I just can't stop stealing things.

Doctor: Well, take these tablets three times a day and if there's no change in a week get me a colour TV and an iPhone.

Son: Dad, can I have another glass of water, please?

Dad: That's the fourth one since you went to bed, why are you so thirsty?

Son: I'm not thirsty, my bedroom's on fire.

What did the woodworm say when he went in the wild west saloon?

Is the bar tender here?

The average age of a child when Dad stops letting them win everything and starts becoming ultra-competitive is 7 years and 2 months.

DAD STAT

'Hello, is that the lunatic asylum?'
'Yes, but I'm afraid we're not on the phone.'

Where do frogs get their eyes tested?
At the hoptician.

Where do frogs leave their coats?
In the croakroom.

What's the difference between a fisherman and a schoolboy?
One baits his hooks and the other hates his books.

What's the most dangerous part of a car?
The nut behind the steering wheel.

I saw Van Gogh in the pub the other day and offered to buy him a drink.
'No thanks,' he said, 'I've got one 'ere.'

Why do birds fly south in the winter?
Because it's too far to walk.

What jumps around belltowers wrapped in clingfilm?
The lunch-pack of Notre Dame.

What happened to the stupid sea scout?
His tent sank.

What happened to the duck who flew upside down?
He quacked up.

Patient: I keep dreaming that I'm covered in gold paint.
Doctor: You obviously have a gilt complex.

Where does the Lone Ranger take his rubbish?
To the dump, to the dump, to the dump,
dump, dump.

Son: Dad, that piece of fish had a bone in it.
Dad: Are you choking?
Son: No, I'm serious.

What happened when the Granny Smith married the Cox's Pippin?
They lived appley ever after.

What is a twack?
Something a twain runs on.

Where do you weigh a whale?
At a whaleway station.

Where do weigh a pie?
Over the rainbow. ('Somewhere over the rainbow, weigh a pie…')

What happened to the snail who lost his shell?
He became very sluggish.

What do you call a man with an exercise bike on his head?
Jim.

What do you call a man with a car on his head?
Jack.

What do worms leave around the rim of their bath?
The scum of the earth.

How do you make a glow-worm happy?
Cut off its tail – it'll be de-lighted.

Why did the viper vipe 'er nose?
Because the adder 'ad 'er 'andkerchief.

How do you confuse a chameleon?
Put him on a tartan rug.

What have Winnie the Pooh and Attila the Hun got in common?
The same middle name.

What do you get if you pour boiling water down a rabbit hole?
Hot cross bunnies.

Why do bees hum?
Because they've forgotten the words.

What time was it when the flea and the fly passed each other?
Fly past flea.

Diner: I'll have a crocodile sandwich, and make it snappy!

What's the maximum sentence for bigamy?
Two mothers-in-law.

First man: My dog's got no nose.
Second man: How does he smell?
First man: Terrible!

First man: I call my dog Isaiah.
Second man: Why do you call your dog Isaiah?
First man: Because one eye's 'igher than the other!

I was just passing a field and heard something go tick-tock, tick-tock, moo, BANG!
It was abominable.

> 𝕬 horse went into a pub. The barman asked him, 'Why the long face?'

Why didn't the skeleton go bungee-jumping?
He didn't have the guts.

Why did the golfer wear two pairs of trousers?
In case he got a hole in one.

What happened to the cowboy who wore paper trousers?
He was done for rustling.

Where do sheep get their hair cut?
At the baa-bers.

Diner: What on earth is this food?

Waiter: It's bean soup, sir.

Diner: I don't want to know what it's been, I want to know what it is now!

Patient: Doctor, people keep ignoring me.

Doctor: Next please.

Patient: Doctor, I keep thinking I'm a mousetrap.

Doctor: Well, snap out of it.

Mum: You've done nothing to help with dinner at all.

Dad: How can you say that? I bought the chicken, plucked it and stuffed it. Now all you've got to do is kill it and put it in the oven.

71% of dads are convinced it doesn't matter what words you sing to a pop song as long as you get the first and last lines right.

DAD STAT

Why did the farmer chase his cow across the bumpy field?
So he could have a milk shake.

Why don't centipedes play football?
By the time they've got their boots on the match is over.

What did the grape say when someone sat on it?
Nothing, it just let out a little whine.

Why do you call your salamander Tiny?
Because he's my newt.

What's black and white and very noisy?
A zebra with a drum kit.

What's black and white and dangerous?
A nun with a submachine-gun.

What happened to the hen who laid the world's largest egg?
She won the Pullet Surprise.

Man: Would you like to play with my new dog?
Boy: He looks very fierce. Does he bite?
Man: That's what I want to find out.

Why does a giraffe have such a long neck?
Because its head is so far from its body.

What do you get hanging from banana trees?
Sore arms!

Diner: Waiter, what's this fly doing in my soup?
Waiter: It looks like the backstroke.

Son: I'm hungry.
Dad: Nice to meet you, Hungry, I'm Dad.

Son: I'm thirsty.
Dad: Hello, Thirsty ... I'm Friday.

How many elephants can you get in a mini?
Four – two in the front and two in the back!

How do you get four giraffes in a mini?
You can't – it's full up with elephants.

I renamed my iPod 'the Titanic' so that when I plug it in iTunes tells me, 'The Titanic is Syncing'.

What did the Buddhist say when he went into the sandwich shop?
Make me one with everything.

What do you call a woman setting fire to her credit card bill?
Bernadette.

Why are pirates, pirates?
Because they ARRRRRRRRRRRRGGGHHH!

Did you hear the one about the magic tractor?
It turned into a field.

What do you call a dinosaur with no eyes?
Doyouthinkhe-saurus.

What's white and blue and if it fell out of a tree would kill you?

A fridge with a denim jacket on.

What's black and white and red all over?

A newspaper.

Doctor: Well, it seems you have what we call 'pedestrian eyes'.

Patient: What's that?

Doctor: They look both ways before they cross.

What is a myth?

A female moth.

What happened when the woman discovered her fiancé had a wooden leg?

She broke it off.

Patient: Doctor, I keep thinking I'm a Welsh pop singer.

Doctor: Ah, you've got Tom Jones syndrome.

Patient: Is that rare?

Doctor: It's not unusual…

What do you call a wizard who kills flies?

Harry Swatter.

What do you call a wizard who makes secret plans?

Harry Plotter.

What do you call a wizard who takes up boxing?

Harry LaMotta.

Why didn't the skeleton go to the party?

Because he had no body to go with.

Patient: Doctor, I can't stop eating snooker balls and it makes me feel terrible. Last night I ate four reds, three pinks and a blue.
Doctor: I can see the trouble. You're not eating your greens.

What did the policeman say to his tummy?
I've got you under a vest.

What flies round lampshades at 100mph?
Stirling Moth.

What goes 'Ooooo, ooooo'?
A ventriloquist cow.

What did the traffic light say to the car?
Don't look, I'm changing.

What do you get if you throw a stick of dynamite into a French flooring shop?

Linoleum Blownapart!

Did you hear about the two antennae who got married?

The ceremony wasn't up to much, but the reception was brilliant.

What do you call a girl with a tortoise on her head?

Shelley.

There are 10 kinds of people in this world — those who understand binary and those who don't.

Fat lady: Can you see me across the road, sonny?

Boy: I could see you from half a mile away!

Why was 6 scared of 7?

Because 7 8 9.

What's hundreds of feet tall and wobbles?

The Trifle Tower.

What time is it when an elephant sits on your fence?

Time to get a new fence.

What goes up when the rain comes down?

An umbrella.

Patient: I keep thinking I'm a cricket ball.

Doctor: How's that?

Patient: Don't you start.

What did the reluctant Australian musician play?
A didgeridon't.

What musical instrument goes best with cheese?
The pickle-o.

Did you hear about the man who bought a paper shop?
It blew away.

Why will you never go hungry in the desert?
Because of all the sand which is there.

Why did the cheese roll?

Because he saw the egg flip.

What did the big chimney say to the little chimney?
You're too young to smoke.

Householder: Will it take you long to fix my window?
Glazier: Well, it's a bigger job than I thought – it's broken on both sides.

What do you call a Russian with a bad cold?
Ivan Astikov.

What's always locked with the keys on the inside?
A piano.

Why is a schoolboy at half-term like a Scotsman with a cold?
They both have a week off.

First man: You shouldn't be patting a pony if you've got a sore throat.
Second man: I'm not patting a pony, I just said I was feeling a little hoarse.

First man: Do you know what good, clean fun is?
Second man: No, what good is it?

Dad: Why does everyone call you the teacher's pet?
Son: She keeps me in a cage.

Where did the policeman live?
Letsby Avenue.

'I want you to tie your horse to that tree and give him some food, do you understand?'
'Oak hay!'

Sergeant: We have a new parachute, men, you wait until you're ten feet from the ground before you pull the cord.

Recruit: What if the parachute doesn't open?

Sergeant: Well, you can jump ten feet, can't you?

What do you call a fly in an idiot's ear?

A space invader.

Who invented fire?

Some bright spark.

Pupil: Are you 32, sir?

Teacher: Why do you ask that?

Pupil: Because my brother's 16 and you're twice as daft as he is.

What are the three most dangerous sports for birds?

Budgie-jumping, hen-gliding and parrot-shooting.

Who was the coldest Roman emperor?
Julius Freezer.

What's a pirate's favourite football team?
Arrrrrrrsenal.

> **What did the biscuit say when it was run over?**
>
> Crumbs!

Why did the environmental lighthouse keeper get the sack?
He kept turning the light off at night.

What do you call Postman Pat when he's been made redundant?
Pat.

> **What the fastest thing at the rubbish tip?**
>
> Stig of the Dump.

What sits around the rubbish tip singing in a funny voice?
Sting of the Dump.

'Here is the forecast for the week ahead. Tomorrow will be Muggy; this will be followed by Tuggy, Weggy, Thuggy and Friggy.'

What do you call a wasp before you kill it?
An isp.

What do you get if you cross a fizzy drink with a marsupial?
Coca-Koala.

Why shouldn't men wear Asian dresses?
Because it's sarong.

What lies on the ground, 100 feet up in the air?
A dead centipede.

What is a deaf lady's favourite letter?
'A', because it makes her hear.

Patient: Doctor, I feel like a pair of scissors.
Doctor: Well, you can cut that out.

How many pigs does it take to make a farmyard smell?

A phew.

What's blue, juicy and cries for help?
A damson in distress.

What do you get if you cross a cow, a sheep and a baby goat?
The milky baa kid.

Two mindreaders met in the street.
One said, 'Hello, you're fine, how am I?'

First sheep: Baa.
Second sheep: Moo.
First sheep: What do you mean, moo?
Second sheep: I'm learning a foreign language.

How does an Eskimo build his house?
Igloos it together.

What's a horse's favourite game?
Stable tennis.

What do you call a donkey with three legs?
A wonkey.

What do you call a donkey with three legs and one eye?
A winky wonkey.

What does a policeman put on his sandwiches?
Truncheon meat.

PE teacher: There are only two things stopping you being a great footballer.
Pupil: Great, what are they?
Teacher: Your left foot and your right foot.

We took Grandad sledging with us but he caught a terrible cold, so Nan rubbed some goosefat all over his chest. He went downhill pretty quick after that.

What do you call a cat that's swallowed a duck?
A duck-filled fatty-puss.

Tourist at top of the Eiffel Tower: Do people fall off here very often? Guide: No, only once.

Son: I've just been to the barber's. Dad: What for, an estimate?

Dad: Don't break wind in front of me, son. Son: Sorry, Dad, I didn't know it was your turn.

Boy: Grandad, can you make a noise like a frog? Grandad: Why do you ask? **Boy: Because Dad says when you croak we're all going to Disneyland.**

What's big, red and lies upside down in the gutter?
A dead bus.

What did the bald man say when he was given a comb for Christmas?
I'll never part with it.

Patient: Doctor, I keep thinking I'm a pack of cards.
Doctor: Shuffle along and I'll deal with you later.

Dad: Whenever I'm down in the dumps I get myself a new tie.
Son: Oh, I wondered where you got them from.

A staggering 96% of dads have no problem with the fact that they heavily edit readings of The Very Hungry Caterpillar and The Gruffalo at bedtime so they don't miss the start of the football on TV (the other 4% do it but feel a tiny bit guilty).

DAD STAT

Patient: Doctor, I've got an awful ache in my right knee.
Doctor: That'll be old age, I'm afraid.
Patient: It can't be – my left knee is just as old, and it doesn't hurt at all.

What relation is a doormat to a doorstep?
A step-farther.

Boy: Dad, why is your face so wrinkly?
Dad: They're not wrinkles, they're laughter lines.
Boy: Trust me, nothing's that funny.

Son: Dad, that ointment you put on my leg's making it smart.
Dad: I'd better rub some on your head, then.

Your mum's teeth are like stars — they come out at night.

What did the Texan say when his dentist told him his teeth were fine?
'Drill anyway, I'm feeling lucky!'

Diner: This food isn't fit for a pig!
Waiter: I'll bring you some that is, sir.

Where do cows go on their day off?
To the moovies.

Why couldn't the idiot play water polo?
His horse kept drowning.

Why do cows lie down in the rain?
To keep each udder warm.

What do you get if cross a pig with a telephone?
A lot of crackling on the line.

What do you call a girl with a frog on her head?
Lily.

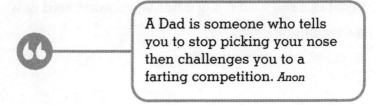

A Dad is someone who tells you to stop picking your nose then challenges you to a farting competition. *Anon*

Why did the runner carry a courgette in each hand?

He was training for the marrowthon.

What are the fastest vegetables?

Runner beans.

What do you call someone who used to like farm machinery?

An ex-tractor fan.

What do you call a man with three dromedaries on his head?

Humphrey.

What do you get if you cross a labrador with a tortoise?
A pet that will fetch you last week's newspaper.

How do you get a baby astronaut to sleep?
Rock-et.

How do you stop your nose from running?
Hide its trainers.

What goes peck, peck, peck, peck, peck, peck, BOOM!?
A chicken in a minefield.

How does a barber cut the man in the moon's hair?
'E clips it.

Why did the lazy parents call their son Six-and-seven-eighths?
They just picked it out of a hat.

Why was the idiot pleased with himself when he finished his jigsaw puzzle?
Because it said '4–6 years' on the box and it only took him three weeks.

Why did the cow cross the road?
To get to the udder side.

Who is the most famous South African in Japan?
Nissan Main Dealer.

Where was the Magna Carta signed?
At the bottom.

What do you call a girl with the Titanic on her head?

Mandy Lifeboats.

Who makes suits and eats spinach?

Popeye the Tailorman.

What happened to the man who invented the door knocker?

He won the no-bell prize.

What's orange and sounds like a parrot?

A carrot.

What happened when a ship carrying red paint collided with a ship carrying brown paint?

Both crews were marooned.

How does Robin call Batman for dinner?
Dinner, dinner, dinner, dinner, dinner, dinner, dinner, dinner, Batman!

Patient: I went glass-blowing this morning and instead of blowing I sucked.
Doctor: So what's the problem?
Patient: I've got a terrible pane in my stomach.

Why couldn't the human cannonball hold down a job?
He kept getting fired.

What's black and white and decimates Europe?
Attila the Nun.

Why couldn't the two elephants go swimming at the same time?
They only had one pair of trunks.

What did the Red Baron say when he bailed out during World War One?
Bi-plane.

Why did the duck cross the road?
It was the chicken's day off.

Patient: Doctor, I keep thinking I'm a goat.
Doctor: How long has this been going on?
Patient: Ever since I was a kid.

Why did the robber take a bar of soap with him when he went to rob the bank?
So he could make a clean getaway.

Customer: Have you got any camouflage jackets?
Assistant: We've got dozens but I can't find them.

What has six legs, is green and fuzzy, and would kill you if it fell on you from a tree?
A snooker table.

What's round and dangerous?
A vicious circle.

What's made of chocolate and lives at the bottom of the sea?
An oyster egg.

What's worse than being with a fool?
Fooling with a bee.

Dad: I was much better at history at school than you are.
Son: Well, there was a lot less of it to learn back then.

If you have a referee in football and an umpire in cricket, what do you have in bowls?
Goldfish.

If King Kong went to Hong Kong to play ping-pong and have a sing-song and died, what would they put on his coffin?
A lid.

Dad: Last night your mum and I fought hammer and tongs.
Son: Who won?
Dad: She did, she had the hammer.

Vet: I'm sorry, but I'm going to have to put your dog down.
Man: But I only brought him in with a bad ear.
Vet: Yes, but he's really heavy.

Why did the cat eat a lump of cheese?
So he could wait by the mousehole with baited breath.

What happened to the frog who stopped on a double-yellow line?
He was toad away.

What do you call a man with scratches on his head?
Claude.

Diner: Waiter, there's a fly in my soup.
Waiter: Yes, sir, our chef used to be a tailor.

Diner: How often do you change the tablecloths here?
Waiter: I don't know, sir, I've only been here six months.

Stupid questions dads ask their kids to catch them out

Who wrote Handel's Messiah? *(Handel)*

How many of each animal did Moses take on the ark?
(None – Noah built the ark)

How many months have 28 days? *(All of them)*

If there are 10 birds on a fence and all but two fly away,
how many are left? *(Two)*

If a train crashed on the England–Scotland border,
where would they bury the survivors?
(You don't bury survivors!)

Doctor: Have you had this problem before?

Patient: Yes, I have.

Doctor: Well, you've got it again.

Patient: Are you sure this ointment will get rid of my spots?

Doctor: Well, I don't like to make rash promises.

What do you call a man with a coat on his head?

Mac.

Why do bagpipers walk while they play?
To get away from the noise.

What do you call a man with two coats on his head?
Max.

What do you call a boomerang that doesn't work?

A stick.

How did the football pitch end up triangle-shaped?

Somebody took a corner.

Why did the footballer take a piece of rope on the pitch?

Because he was the skipper.

Diner: Waiter, this soup tastes funny.

Waiter: Then why aren't you laughing?

Dad: What do you mean by telling all your mates I'm an idiot?

Son: I'm sorry, I didn't know it was a secret.

Mum: Tell me what Dad said when he hit his thumb with the hammer, but leave out the naughty words.

Son: In that case he didn't say anything.

How do you cure a headache?
Put your head through a window and the pane will disappear.

What's the difference between a set of bagpipes and an onion?
No one cries when you chop up a set of bagpipes.

Patient: Doctor, I think I've got déjà vu?

Doctor: Didn't I see you yesterday?

What do you get when you cross a thief with an orchestra?

Robbery with violins.

What did the scarf say to the hat?
You go on ahead and I'll hang around.

Did you hear about the butcher who backed into the bacon slicer?
He got a little behind in his work.

Why did the mushroom get invited to lots of parties?
Because he was a fun guy.

Doctor: You'll need stitches in that cut.
Patient: Don't you bother, I'll do it.
Doctor: Suture self.

Did you hear about the jockey who was hit by a turkey, a tin of salmon and a Christmas pudding while he was racing?
He complained to the stewards that he'd been hampered.

Why did the art thief's van run out of petrol as he drove away from the Louvre?
Because he had no Monet to buy Degas to make the Van Gogh.

What did one tonsil say to the other?
Get dressed, the doctor's taking us out tonight.

Mum: Why did you send my son home from school?

Head: He was weeing in the swimming pool.

Mum: All little boys do that.

Head: Not from the diving board, they don't.

Why was early history called the Dark Ages?

Because there were so many knights.

What has four wheels and flies?

A rubbish lorry.

How did Vikings communicate?

In Norse Code.

If at first you don't succeed, don't try sky-diving.

What do you get if you cross a dog with a tiger?

A very nervous postman.

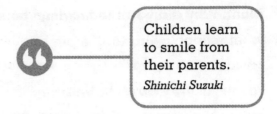

Children learn to smile from their parents.
Shinichi Suzuki

'Doctor, I think I need glasses.'
'You certainly do, this is a fish and chip shop.'

Where do baby gorillas sleep?

In an ape-ri-cot.

Teacher: You missed school yesterday, didn't you?
Pupil: Not very much.

Two flies were playing football in a saucer when the team captain came over to watch them. He told them, 'You'll have to do better than that tomorrow, we're playing in the cup.'

I can only remember 25 letters of the alphabet. I don't know why.

What did the inflatable headmaster say to the inflatable boy who took a pin into his inflatable school?
You've let me down, you've let the school down, but most of all you've let yourself down.

Why are zombies never lonely?
They can always dig up a few friends.

What do vampires cross the sea in?
Blood vessels.

What do you call a woman with one leg shorter than the other?
Eileen.

Diner: Waiter, your thumb is in my soup.
Waiter: Don't worry, sir, it's not hot.

What's yellow, flat and flies around the kitchen?
An unidentified flying omelette.

Patient: I've got water on the brain, what can you do about it?
Doctor: What you need is a tap on the head.

What goes ha-ha-ha bonk?
A man laughing his head off.

Patient: Doctor, when I stand up too quickly I see Mickey Mouse and Donald Duck.
Doctor: And how long have you been having these Disney spells?

What do you do when your nose goes on strike?
Picket.

What's got four legs and an arm?
A contented Rottweiler.

Patient: Doctor, I've just swallowed some Christmas decorations.
Doctor: Ah, you've got tinselitis.

Patient: Doctor, I seem to be getting smaller and smaller.
Doctor: Well, you'll just have to be a little patient.

Diner: Waiter, there's a dead fly in my soup.
Waiter: Yes, sir, it's the hot water that kills them.

What goes 99-clonk, 99-clonk?

A centipede with a wooden leg.

What has 50 legs but can't walk?

Half a centipede.

What did dinosaurs have that no other animals had?
Baby dinosaurs.

What did the optimist say when he fell from the top of a skyscraper and passed the tenth floor?
So far, so good.

Diner: Why have you got your thumb on my sandwich?
Waiter: I don't want it to fall on the floor again.

What happened when two balls of string had a race?
It ended in a tie.

How do you make anti-freeze?
Hide her nightie.

Teacher: I hope I didn't see you copying in that test.
Pupil: I hope you didn't, either.

Teacher: If you multiplied 5,789 by 2,393, what answer would you get?
Pupil: The wrong one.

What do you call a man with a number plate on his head?
Reg.

Dad: You've got your shoes on the wrong feet, son.
Son: But these are the only feet I've got.

What's green, has pips and conquers Asia Minor?
Alexander the Grape.

Why couldn't the sailor play cards?
The captain was standing on the deck.

How do you use an Egyptian doorbell?

Just toot and come in.

Why did the chewing gum cross the road?
It was stuck to the chicken's foot.

What do you call a vicar on a motorbike?
Rev.

What's ten feet tall, green and sits in the corner all night?
The Incredible Sulk.

What did the Spanish farmer say to his chickens?
Oh, lay!

What did the alien say to the petrol pump?
Take your finger out of your ear when I'm talking to you.

Patient: Doctor, I've got a bit of lettuce sticking out of my ear.
Doctor: Oh dear, I think that's just the tip of an iceberg.

Why was the chicken sent home from school?
For using fowl language.

Patient: Doctor, I've just swallowed my mouth organ.
Doctor: Thank goodness you don't play the piano.

Teacher: How did you get that black eye?
Pupil: You see that tree on the school field?
Teacher: Yes.
Pupil: I didn't.

What should you do if you keep getting emails saying, 'What's up, doc?'
Check for Bugs in your system.

What kind of animal has four legs and can see just as well from both ends?

A dog with his eyes closed.

Teacher: What does it mean when the smoke alarm goes off?
Pupil: In our house, it means dinner's ready.

Diner: Waiter, there's no chicken in my chicken pie.
Waiter: Well, there's no shepherd in the shepherd's pie either.

Diner: I know I'm in a hurry, but I'd like to know why my pie is so flat?
Waiter: You said, 'Get me a pie and step on it.'

What's orange and invisible?
No carrots.

What else is black and white and red all over?
A nun with a nosebleed.

What's black and white and red all over?
A sunburned penguin.

What did the football manager do when the pitch flooded?
He brought the subs on.

Pupil: I don't think I deserve zero for this test, sir.
Teacher: Neither do I, but it's the lowest I can give you.

What's yellow and square?
A banana that's into classical music.

What do you give birds when they're ill?
Tweetment.

A couple went to a fancy-dress party in a barcode costume.
They'd decided they were an item.

What happened to the shoplifter who stole a calendar?
He got twelve months.

How does Good King Wenceslas like his pizzas?
Deep-pan, crisp and even.

Diner: Waiter, this coffee tastes like mud.
Waiter: Well, it was ground only this morning.

Did you hear that the world's most annoying practical joker has just been buried?
He isn't dead, it's just the neighbours getting their own back.

Why did it take so long to get the man who wrote the Hokey-Cokey into his coffin when he died?
Well, first they put his left arm in ...

An Englishman, an Irishman and a Scotsman walked into a pub.
The barman said, 'Is this some kind of joke?'

A gorilla went into a pub and ordered a pint of beer.
'That'll be £6.50, please,' said the barman, adding, 'We don't get many gorillas in here.'
The gorilla said, 'I'm not surprised at £6.50 a pint.'

What do you call a fly with no wings?
A walk.

How do you hire a horse?

Put a brick under each hoof.

Did you hear about the actor who fell through a trapdoor?
It was just a stage he was going through.

Actor: Have you seen me on TV?
Fan: On and off.
Actor: How did you like me?
Fan: Off.

Two caterpillars were crawling along a leaf when a butterfly flew past.
One said to the other, 'You'll never get me up in one of those things.'

What did the duck say when she bought some lipstick?

Put it on my bill.

A sloth was mugged by four snails.
The policeman asked him if he could remember much about the incident.
'Not really, it all happened so fast.'

Why is Turtle Wax so expensive?
Because turtles have really small ears.

Why did the baker stop making doughnuts?
He got fed up of the hole business.

What's white, fluffy and beats its chest?
A meringue-utan.

How do porcupines play leapfrog?
Very carefully.

What goes 'Oh, oh, oh!'?
Santa walking backwards.

Why is an icy pavement musical?
If you don't c-sharp you'll b-flat.

What do bees do with their honey?
They cell it.

How do you turn vegetable soup into golden vegetable soup?
Add 24 carrots.

Doctor: I'm afraid your condition is terminal and I only expect you to live another ten –
Patient: Months? Weeks!? Days!!!?
Doctor: Nine, eight, seven, six ...

Why did the man with no alarm clock sleep under his car?
He wanted to wake up oily in the morning.

When do ghosts usually appear?
Just before someone screams.

What do you get if you cross an egg with a stick of dynamite with a piece of wood?
A boom-meringue.

What part of a fish weighs the most?

The scales.

Why do seagulls fly over the sea?
Because if they flew over the bay they'd be bagels.

What do you call a man with a rabbit on his head?
Warren.

Who serves ice cream faster than a speeding bullet?
Scooperman!

Why didn't the bike go for a swim?

It was two-tyred.

Is it hard to spot a leopard?

No, they're born like that.

What do you get if you cross a sheep with a porcupine?
An animal that knits its own jumpers.

Why did the spider go on the computer?
He was looking for a web site.

Why isn't your nose twelve inches long?
Because then it would be a foot.

Son: Dad, will you do my maths homework for me tonight?
Dad: No, son, it wouldn't be right.
Son: Well, just do your best.

Dad: Why are you home from school early?

Son: I was the only one who could answer a question.

Dad: What was the question?

Son: 'Who broke that window?'

Man to chemist: Can you make me something up quickly?

Chemist: Of course. And did you know the Queen was in here yesterday?

Man: Was she really?

Chemist: No, I just made it up.

Baby snake: Mum, am I venomous?

Mummy snake: No, dear.

Baby snake: Thank goodness for that, I've just bitten my tongue.

First cow: So, what do you think about this mad cow disease?

Second cow: Why should I care, I'm Napoleon.

Are deep-sea divers with chicken pox any good?
Well, they certainly come up to scratch.

What's the difference between roast potatoes and pea soup?
Anyone can roast potatoes.

How do you make holy water?
Boil the hell out of it.

A set of jump leads went into a pub and asked for a drink.
The barman said, 'OK, but don't go starting anything.'

Two cannibals were eating a clown.
One said to the other, 'Does this taste funny to you?'

The invisible man married the invisible woman and they had a daughter. She wasn't much to look at, either.

A peanut ran into the police station.

'I've just been a salted.'

Son: **Dad, how much does it cost to get married?**
Dad: I don't know, I haven't finished paying yet.

Son: **Mum's moaning that you never take her anywhere expensive.**
Dad: That's rubbish, I took her to the petrol station yesterday.

Doctor: **Well, your test results came back negative.**
Patient: That's good, isn't it?
Doctor: **Not really, it was an IQ test.**

A cheese sandwich walked into a pub and asked for a drink.
The barman said, 'I'm sorry, we don't serve food here.'

I want to die peacefully in my sleep like my dad.
Not screaming and terrified like his passengers.

Son: Why do you call Dad 'Slinky'?
Mum: Well, he's not much use for anything but I can't help smiling when he falls down the stairs.

Son: Why does Dad call his desk his 'work station'?
Mum: Well, a bus station is where a bus stops, a train station is where a train stops, so …

What do you call a gun with three barrels?

A trifle.

How much did it cost the pirate to get his ears pierced?
A buck an ear.

Why did the grape go out with the plum?
Because he couldn't get a date.

Why did the keen footballer join the submarine service?
He heard there were 20,000 leagues under the sea.

A sausage and a rasher of bacon were in a frying pan and the sausage said, 'Gosh, it's hot in here,' and the bacon said, 'Wow, a talking sausage!'

First pirate: How come you've got a hook instead of a hand and an eyepatch instead of an eye?

Second pirate: A shark bit my hand off and a seagull pooped in my eye.

First pirate: You lost your eye because of seagull poop?

Second pirate: Well, it was my first day with the hook.

What do you call a missing parrot?

A polygon.

What's the difference between a fly and a mosquito?

A mosquito can fly but a fly can't mosquito.

Patient: Doctor, some days I feel like I'm a wigwam, and other days I feel like I'm a marquee.

Doctor: Your problem is you're two tents.

Why do ducks have webbed feet?

To stamp out forest fires.

Why do elephants have flat feet?

To stamp out flaming ducks.

Patient: Doctor, I keep thinking I'm a bell.
Doctor: Take these tablets and if they don't work give me a ring.

Last night I dreamed I was eating a giant marshmallow.
When I woke up this morning I couldn't find my pillow.

What did an annoyed Captain Kirk say to his chief engineer?
'Very funny, Scottie. Now beam up my clothes.'

First ant: What's that smell, is it you?

Second ant: No, it's de oder ant.

> **What do you call an ape in a minefield?**
>
> A baboom.

What are caterpillars afraid of?

Dogerpillars.

A fat man and a thin man were walking in the mountains when they were surprised by a grizzly bear. The thin man started to run.

'It's useless,' shouted the fat man. 'No one can outrun a grizzly.'

'I don't need to outrun the grizzly,' called back his friend, 'I just need to outrun you.'

Why did the farmer win the Nobel Prize?
He was out standing in his field.

What did one eye say to the other?
Between you and me, something smells.

Which side of a duck has the most feathers?
The outside.

How many seconds are there in a year?
Twelve (January 2nd, February 2nd, March 2nd …).

Patient: Doctor, every time I drink a cup of coffee I get a pain in my nose.
Doctor: Try taking out the spoon first.

Patient: Doctor, I think I'm a moth.
Doctor: Well, you really need to see a psychiatrist.
Patient: I know, but I was passing your surgery and your light was on ...

An idiot dashed into the police station.
'My car's just been stolen, but don't worry, I got the registration number.'

What kind of lights did Noah have in the ark?

Floodlights.

What do you call an idiot under a wheelbarrow?
A mechanic.

Teacher: What's your name?

New boy: Reginald Michael Dipstick.

Teacher: I'll just put down 'Reginald Dipstick'.

New boy: My dad won't like that – he hates it when people take the mickey out of my name.

Who made King Arthur's round table?

Sir Cumference.

Dad: I've just been told you skipped school to play football.

Son: I didn't and I've got the cinema ticket to prove it.

Why didn't Noah catch many fish from the ark?

He only had two worms.

Son: I got into trouble at school today because I didn't know where my adenoids were.

Dad: Well, you should remember where you put things.

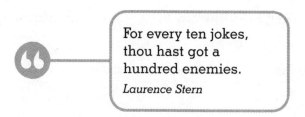

For every ten jokes, thou hast got a hundred enemies.
Laurence Stern

Diner: Waiter, could you tell me exactly what's in this dish, please?

Waiter: Do you want the recipe?

Diner: No, I just want to know the ingredients in case the doctor asks me.

What language do Cubans speak?

Cubic.

What was Camelot famous for?

Its knight life.

How many balls of string would it take to reach the moon?

One if it was long enough.

Why did the Scotsman eat his pudding with his main course?

So he could have tart'n'chips.

How was the Roman Empire cut in half?

With a pair of Caesars.

What do you call a mountain with hiccups?

A volcano.

Rambler: Will this path take me to the main road?

Farmer: No, you'll have to go by yourself.

Boy: I wish I had enough money to buy an elephant.

Girl: What do you want an elephant for?

Boy: I don't, I just wish I had the money.

Tonto: Bad news, Kimo Sabe. There are Sioux behind us, Arapaho to the left of us, Cheyenne to the right of us and Cherokee in front of us.

Lone Ranger: Well, old friend, it looks like the end of the line for us.

Tonto: Speak for yourself, Paleface.

How many ants do you need to fill a rented flat?
Ten ants.

How do Welsh people eat cheese?

Caerphilly.

Patient: Doctor, I've had this terrible pain in my stomach since I ate crab yesterday.

Doctor: Did it smell bad when you took it out of its shell?

Patient: What do you mean, 'took it out of its shell'?

Patient: Doctor, I keep thinking I'm a dog.

Doctor: Lie down on the couch and I'll see what I can do.

Patient: But I'm not allowed on the couch.

Teacher: Name five animals that you'd find in Australia?

Pupil: Er, a koala, a crocodile and three kangaroos.

Why did the owl 'owl?
Because the woodpecker would peck 'er.

How do we know that owls are cleverer than chickens?
Have you ever heard of Kentucky Fried Owl?

What bird is always out of breath?
A puffin.

What do you get if you cross a parrot with a woodpecker?
A bird that talks in Morse code.

What does a caterpillar do on New Year's Day?
Turns over a new leaf.

What's bright red and weighs four tons?
An elephant holding its breath.

What do you call a girl with a tennis racket on her head?
Annette.

Three brothers bought a cattle ranch, but couldn't agree on what to name it, so they asked their dad. 'Call it "Focus",' he said. When they asked why he said, 'Because it's where the sons raise meat.'

Teacher: How do you spell 'education'?
Pupil: E-D-D-U-K-A-Y-S-H-U-N.
Teacher: That's not how the dictionary spells it.
Pupil: You didn't ask me how the dictionary spells it.

Patient: Doctor, when I get up in the morning I'm very dizzy for half an hour.
Doctor: Well, you should get up half an hour later.

What fish makes you an offer you can't refuse?

The Cod Father.

A golfer is practising and knocking ball after ball into the lake.

'You should practise with old balls,' said his partner.

'I never have any balls long enough for them to get old!'

The man who walked into the bar earlier (remember him?) was knocked unconscious and came round in hospital to find a nurse standing over him.

'Have I come here to die?' he asked.

'No,' said the nurse, 'you came here yesterdie.'

Son: Dad, can we go to Wembley to watch England play?

Dad: No, they never came to see me when I was bad.

What happened when someone gave an idiot a pair of water skis?
He spent the rest of his life trying to find a lake with a slope on it.

Patient: Doctor, I can't stop breaking wind.
Doctor: Right, pass me that long pole with the hook on it and drop your trousers.
Patient: What on earth are you going to do?
Doctor: Well, for a start I'm going to open the window.

Two fleas were dashing across the top of a soup packet.
'Why are we going so fast?' asked one.
'Can't you read?' said the other. 'It says "tear along the dotted line".'

What kind of noise annoys an oyster?

A noisy noise annoys an oyster.

What's green, sooty, and whistles when it rubs its back legs together?
Chimney Cricket.

A brain walks into a pub and asks for a pint of beer.
'I'm not serving you,' said the barman, 'you're out of your head already.'

Teacher: Why weren't you in school yesterday?
Pupil: My grandad got burned, Miss.
Teacher: Not badly, I hope.
Pupil: Well, they don't mess about at the crematorium.

Teacher: If Elvis Presley were alive today, what would he be doing?
Pupil: Trying to get out of his coffin, sir.

Patient: Doctor,
I've broken my
arm in two places.
Doctor: Well you
shouldn't have gone
to those places.

What do you call a
swimmer with no
arms and no legs?

Bob.

Patient: Doctor, wherever I touch myself on my
body it really hurts.
Doctor: That's because you've got a broken finger.

Child: Dad, our Jimmy's spoilt.
Dad: He certainly is not.
Child: Suit yourself, but wait till you see what the
steamroller's done to him.

DAD STAT

The average 40-year-old
Dad will have 30% less
hair than his childless
counterpart – and twice
as much of it will be grey.

Did you hear about the pizza delivery man who was found dead in his car covered in olives, peppers and ground beef?
The police think he topped himself.

What did the doctor say to the man covered in clingfilm?
I can clearly see you're nuts.

Did you know they played tennis in the Bible?
It says Joseph served in Pharaoh's court.

What's small, brown and carries a suitcase?

A handle.

Patient: Doctor, I keep seeing an insect spinning in front of my eyes.

Doctor: Yes, there's a bug going round.

Patient: Since you fitted these false teeth I can't pronounce my f's and th's properly.

Dentist: Well, you can't say fairer than that then.

Man: I say, your dog just ate my hat.

Dog-owner: That's not my problem.

Man: Well, I must say I don't like your attitude.

Dog-owner: Yes, but it was your 'at 'e chewed, not mine.

Doctor: What seems to be the problem?

Patient: It's my head, doctor, I've had it on and off for years.

What should you do if you tread on a moth?
Just wipe it off your shoe, of course.

The worst team in the league finally managed to win a match.
'Shall we do a lap of honour?' asked one player.
'No, just shake hands with the crowd, it'll be quicker.'

Judge: I was going to give you six months, but I have a feeling I've seen your face before.
Defendant: Yes, your honour, I gave your son violin lessons last year.
Judge: So you did. Five years, then!

Son: Mum, Dad's gone out.
Mum: Put a bit more petrol on him, then.

What should you do if you tread on a mouse?
Give it mouth-to-mouse resuscitation.

Doctor: Did the medicine I gave your wife straighten her out?
Man: It certainly did, we buried her yesterday.

Why did the terrible musician hang around outside his house?
He couldn't find the key and didn't know when to come in anyway.

Why shouldn't you drive a mini off a cliff with three bagpipe players in it?
Because you could fit at least one more in.

Examiner: What do you do at a red light?
Driver: Well, to be honest, I normally pick my nose.

Why was the stupid athlete disqualified?
He won the 20km walk for three years running.

How can you get four suits for just a pound?
Buy a pack of cards.

What did the zero say to the eight?
Nice belt!

What does a clock do when it's hungry?
Goes back four seconds.

What do you find in an empty nose?
Fingerprints.

Teacher: Which two days begin with 'T'?
Pupil: Today and tomorrow.

What do you call a dog with no legs?
You can call him whatever you like, but he's not going to come.

Passenger: Does this bus go to Watford?
Bus driver: No.
Passenger: It says 'Watford' on the front.
Bus driver: It says 'India' on the tyres but we're not going there either.

Why did the football manager feed his team on dog food?

He wanted them to win a lot.

An idiot walked into a library and said, 'Fish and chips, please!'
'I'm sorry, sir, but this is a library.'
'Sorry,' whispered the idiot, 'fish and chips, please.'

Teacher: What's half of 8?
Pupil: Horizontally or vertically?
Teacher: What's the difference?
Pupil: Well, horizontally it's 0, vertically it's 3.

How do you turn a duck into a soul singer?
Put it in a microwave until its bill withers.

What do you call someone who hangs around musicians?

A drummer.

Son: Why are you staring at that carton of orange juice?
Dad: Because it says 'concentrate'.

What's the difference between a tea bag and a terrible football team?
A teabag stays in the cup for longer.

Teacher: How long has your father been in his current position?
Pupil: Three months.
Teacher: And what is he doing?
Pupil: Six months.

Teacher: If you had one rabbit in a hutch and added another rabbit, how many rabbits would you have?

Pupil: Ten.

Teacher: Ten? You don't know much about arithmetic.

Pupil: You don't know much about rabbits.

Where were you born?

Birmingham.

What part?

All of me.

Have many great people been born there?
No, just babies.

Have you lived there all your life?
Not yet.

Rambler: That's a lovely windmill you have there.
Farmer: Arrr, we used to have two, but we knocked one down as there wasn't enough wind.

What do you get if you drop a piano on an army base?
A flat major.

How do you mend a broken tuba?
With a tuba glue.

Where do you find a horse with no legs?
Wherever you left him.

What do you call 100 sets of bagpipes at the bottom of the sea?

A good start.

Teacher: Johnny, when's your birthday?

Pupil: May 12th.

Teacher: Which year?

Pupil: Every year.

Why are elephants so wrinkly?

Have you ever tried to iron one?

Why do cemeteries have a wall around them?

Because people are dying to get in.

Why did they bury the pole vaulter at the top of a hill?

Because he was dead.

Patient: Doctor, I'm all mixed up.

Doctor: Why do you say that?

Patient: Well, my nose is running and my feet smell.

How many chimneys does Santa have to climb down on Christmas Eve?
Stacks.

How do lizards find each other?
Gecko location.

Did you hear about the forgetful Aborigine?
He couldn't remember how to throw his boomerang, but then it came back to him.

What do you do when a chicken has toothache?
Pullet.

What do you call a girl with sausage and burgers on her head?
Barbie.

What's yellow and stupid?

Thick custard.

What's yellow, frothy, and throws itself off the edge of the table?

Lemming meringue.

How did the magician cut the sea in half?

He used a sea saw.

Why did the baby biscuit cry?

Because its mother had been a wafer so long.

Why is the sky so high?

So the birds don't bump their heads.

What's brown, smelly and sounds like a bell?

Dung!

144

Five reasons why you shouldn't trust men who *were* dads:

1. Josef Stalin: had a son who tried to shoot himself because he felt so unloved – he failed. His father's reaction? 'He can't even shoot straight.'

2. Ismail Ibn Sharif: known for his penchant for displaying vanquished enemies' heads on the walls of his city, and said to have fathered over 1,000 children ... bet he never remembered their birthdays.

3. Peter the Great: had his son and heir tortured to death when he suspected him of treason.

4. Abraham: was willing to sacrifice his son Isaac until God told him it was all a wind-up – I bet Isaac looked at Dad in a new light after that.

5. Vlad the Impaler: As if being notorious for his ingenious ways of torturing and executing people weren't bad enough, what sort of Dad calls his son Dracula? That's nearly as bad as Harper Seven.

What green and red and goes round and round?
Kermit in a food processor.

Why couldn't anyone get through to the pirate on his phone?
He'd left it off the hook.

Patient: Nurse, I can't feel my legs.
Nurse: That's because we've amputated your arms.

Son: Mum, Dad says I got all my intelligence from him.

Mum: He must be right, because I still have mine.

An idiot rings a travel agent and asks, 'Can you tell me how long it will take to fly from London to New York?'

'Just a minute,' said the travel agent.

'Thanks,' said the idiot, and hung up.

Son: Dad, give me three good reasons why I have to go to school today.

Dad: Firstly, everyone will miss you. Secondly, think of all the work you'll have to catch up. And thirdly, you're the headmaster.

It was the annual nuns v. monks darts match. A monk went first and scored treble 20, single 20, then his third dart hit the wire and bounced out, hitting a nun right between the eyes and killing her. What did the scorer say?

'One nun dead and eighty!'

Pupil: Our dog bit three people yesterday so we had him put down.

Teacher: Was he mad?

Pupil: Well, he wasn't very happy.

Doctor: You've broken your fingers but we'll be able to sort you out.

Patient: Will I be able to play the piano when they're better?

Doctor: Certainly you will.

Patient: That's great, because I couldn't before.

What do you call a snake in the Canadian police?

Mountie Python.

Son: Dad, I woke up laughing this morning.
Dad: You must have slept funny.

Son: Dad, where was I born?
Dad: In hospital.
Son: Why, was I ill?

> **Why didn't the owl take his girlfriend out in the rain?**
>
> It was too wet to woo.

Why do people take an instant dislike to the bagpipes?
It saves time.

Who was the most specialised doctor in the military hospital?
The naval surgeon.

What do nuclear scientists eat for dinner?
Fission chips.

Which soldier puts everyone to sleep?
General Anaesthetic.

Who's the cleverest soldier?
General Knowledge.

And the worst?
Major Disaster.

And the nosiest?
Private Eye.

What gruesome discovery did they find in Uncle Tom's cabin?
Harriet Beecher's toe.

Who hung around Victorian London taking his clothes off?
Jack the Stripper.

Son: Mum, can we get Dad a round tuit for his birthday?

Mum: What on earth is a round tuit?

Son: I don't know, but he says he'll fix my bike when he gets one.

Where do you bury an LP?

The vinyl resting place.

> **Where do fish go dancing?**
> At the fishcoteque.

What happened when the Chinese zoo ran out of bamboo?

There was panda-monium.

What do you call a German barber?

Herr Kutz.

Why shouldn't a fruit marry a vegetable?

Because their children might be melon-cauli.

What's 180 feet high, made of cheese and tomato and is about to fall over?

The leaning tower of pizza.

Why did the Chinese chef spend so long in the kitchen?

He was a wokaholic.

What did the magician say when he produced a skewer of meat from his top hat?

Abra-kebab-ra.

An idiot fell into a vat of beer at the brewery today and drowned.

How do you know he was an idiot?

He got out twice to go to the toilet.

What do you call a chicken on rollerskates?

Poultry in motion.

The average length of time between becoming a first-time Dad and your youngest leaving home is 25 years, 3 months and 4 days (not that I'm counting...)

DAD STAT

Where did Robin Hood buy his flowers?
Sherwood Florist.

Hotelier: It's £50 a night but £25 if you make your own bed.
Guest: I don't mind making my own bed.
Hotelier: Good, I'll just get you the hammer and nails and some wood.

What happened to the dyslexic devil-worshipper?
He sold his soul to Santa.

Did you hear about the man who lost his left arm, left leg and left eye in an accident?
He's all right now.

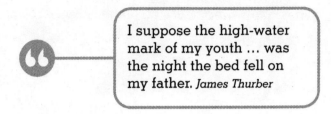

I suppose the high-water mark of my youth ... was the night the bed fell on my father. *James Thurber*

I saw a cricket ball in the sky and kept wondering why it was getting bigger.

And then it hit me...

Customer: Is this insecticide good for ants?

Assistant: No! It kills them!

Grandad: I remember when I could go down to the shops with a pound note and come back with all my shopping for the week. I can't do that now.

Grandson: No, not since they put in all those surveillance cameras.

What's ET short for?

Because he's only got little legs.

What happened to the hyena who swallowed an Oxo cube?
He made a laughing stock of himself.

What's a wok?
Something you thwow at a wabbit.

What's the difference between a Brussels sprout and a bogey?
Have you tried getting kids to eat sprouts?

What do you call a woman tied to the riverbank?
Maud.

Diner: I'll have the tarka masala, please.

Waiter: Don't you mean the tikka masala?

Diner: No, it's similar but a little 'otter.

Two monkeys are in a bath.

One goes, 'Oooh! Oooh! Oooh!'

The other says, 'Put some more cold water in then.'

Son: Was your wedding very emotional?

Dad: I'll say. Even the cake was in tiers.

The local wig shop has been burgled.

Police are combing the area.

What did the letter say to the stamp?

Stick with me and we'll go places.

Why didn't anyone feel sorry for the donkey who ate too many thistles?
Eeyore to have known better.

Where do cars go to play?
The car park, of course.

What flies after criminals and wobbles?
A police jellycopter.

Patient: Doctor, I've got a scone stuck in my ear.
Doctor: Don't worry, I've got some cream for that.

What do you call a Frenchman wearing sandals?
Phillipe Felop.

Idiot: Every time I fill the bath you sold me all the water drains away.
DIY assistant: Have you got a plug?
Idiot: I didn't even know it needed electricity.

What should you do if an idiot throws a pin at you?
Run for it – he's got a hand grenade in his mouth.

Dad: Did you hear about the cornflake who was out for a drive one day when his car lost control? He swerved off the road, crashed through a fence, tore over a field and was heading for a cliff edge when...
Son: Well, what happened?
Dad: I'll tell you next week, it's a cereal.

What did the cannibals do after the wedding?
Toasted the happy couple.

What do you call a man with a load of hay on his head?

Rick.

Policeman: Excuse me. Sir, this is a one-way street.
Motorist: That's all right, I'm only going one way.

What's the fastest cake in the world?
'S'gone.

What did the policeman order in the restaurant?
Irish Stew, in the name of the law.

Dad: Why haven't you washed your hair?
Son: I was going to but the shampoo bottle said
'for dry hair' and mine was already wet.

An idiot was waiting at a bus stop when his friend came up in a car.

'Do you want a lift?' he asked.

'I'd better not, I might miss my bus.'

A man was in a hot-air balloon but had lost his bearings. Seeing a farmer in a field below, he shouted out, 'Where am I?'

'You can't fool me,' said the farmer, 'you're in that basket.'

Science teacher: If you are in a vacuum and call out your name, will you hear it?

Pupil: That depends whether it's on or off.

Dad: Do you want to see the world's fastest magic trick?

Son: Go on then.

Dad: Do you want to see it again?

Pupil: My hamster died last night, miss, so Dad cooked it up with some sugar and fed it to the dog, but he wouldn't eat it so Dad buried it in the garden. When I got up this morning there were some lovely tulips growing there.

Teacher: I find that hard to believe.

Pupil: Haven't you heard of 'tulips from hamster jam'?

First idiot (looking at the moon): Do you think it's further to France or the moon?

Second idiot: What a stupid question. You can't even see France from here.

How does the Pope pay for things on eBay?

He uses his papal account.

Why did the girl put make-up on her forehead?

She was trying to make up her mind.

Son: Dad, I'm having trouble getting into the Harry Potter books, they're too unbelievable.

Dad: Well, lots of books have magic and flying broomsticks in them.

Son: Oh, that doesn't bother me – but a ginger kid with two friends?!

Why do French people never eat more than one egg at a time?

Because one egg is un oeuf.

Where did the fake blacksmith work?

The forgery.

What's the richest fruit in the world?

The sultana Brunei.

DAD STAT

A recent scientific study showed the five stages of fatherhood from conception to birth to be: shock, elation, worry, relief, joy. The five stages of fatherhood from birth to adulthood were similarly proved to be: worry, worry, worry, worry, panic!

What happened when a team of English artists played a team of French artists at football?
It ended in a draw.

An Englishman, an Irishman, a Scotsman and a doctor went into a pub.
The doctor said, 'I'm awfully sorry, I seem to be in the wrong joke.'

Dustman: Where's your bin?
Man: I've bin on holiday.
Dustman: No, where's your wheely bin?
Man: I've weally bin on holiday, honest.

Doctor: I'm afraid you'll have to stop tap-dancing.
Patient: Why?
Doctor: Because I'm trying to examine you.

What did the cat say when he hijacked the plane?
Take me to the Canaries.

> **What's the hottest letter in the alphabet?**
>
> 'B', because it makes oil boil.

Pupil: Are you sure this recipe's right?

Cookery teacher: Pineapples, three cubed – what's wrong with that?

Pupil: Well, 27 pineapples seems an awful lot for one fruit salad.

What does an actor say when he gets into work?

Do you want fries with that?

Teacher: As you're new here, I want you to know that I'm very strict and I only call boys by their surnames. What's your full name?

Pupil: Robert Sweetie.

Teacher: Very well, Robert, just take a seat at the back.

What happened to the man who was running in front of a car?
He soon got tyred, so he got back up and ran behind the car and then he was exhausted.

What's the difference between ignorance and indifference?
I don't know and I don't care!

What happens to people who say 'flipping' and 'flaming'?
They go to heck.

What happened when there was a siege at the Met Office?
Police stormed the building.

Applicant: If I get the job will I be paid weekly or monthly?
Boss: I guarantee you'll be paid weakly.

Why wouldn't the wallpaper talk to the clothes line?

It was too stuck up to hang out with him.

Why did the decorator put an extra jacket on to paint the wall?

Because the tin said it would need two coats.

What should you do if you split your sides laughing?

Run until you get a stitch.

What should you do if you're offered a plate of Mum's rock cakes?

Take your pick.

Two fishermen were out in their boat when a hand appeared out of the water and moved from side to side before disappearing.

'Do you think that was someone drowning?' asked one.

'No,' said his friend, 'it was just a little wave.'

What do you call a man with a large flat fish on his head?

Ray.

What do you call a man without a large flat fish on his head?

X-Ray.

Sooty and Sweep robbed a bank yesterday.

Police believe Matthew Corbett had a hand in it.

Dad: Had you heard they're not going to grow bananas any longer?

Son: Oh no, why not?

Dad: Because they're long enough already.

Judge: What is your occupation?

Defendant: A locksmith, your honour.

Judge: And what were you doing in the bank at 1 a.m. when the police entered?

Defendant: I was making a bolt for the door.

Did you hear about the idiot who hijacked a submarine?

He demanded ten million pounds and a parachute.

Who lost a herd of elephants?

Big Bo Peep.

How do you confuse an idiot?

Put three shovels against a wall and tell him to take his pick.

> **What happened to the karate black belt who joined the army?**
> He nearly killed himself the first time he saluted.

Boy: I'd like some birdseed, please.
Shop assistant: And how many birds do you have?
Boy: None yet, I'm going to grow some.

Dad: Would you like a pocket calculator for Christmas, son?
Son: No thanks, I already know how many pockets I've got.

Son: Dad, have you got holes in your underpants?
Dad: No, of course not!
Son: Then how do you get your feet through?

Five reasons why you shouldn't trust men who *weren't* dads:

1. Immanuel Kant: Gloomy philosopher who apparently never travelled more than 10 miles from his birthplace in his entire life – this did not stop him pontificating to us all on how we should live our lives, so maybe he should have been a dad after all.

2. Cliff Richard: just think how many songs he wouldn't have recorded if he'd been changing nappies and thinking up awful jokes to 'entertain' his kids with.

3. Robespierre: driving force behind the French Revolution's notorious Reign of Terror, during which thousands of people lost their lives.

4. Dr Seuss: I'm sure you don't need me to tell you that he wrote in anapestic tetrameter in order to take colossal amounts of money from dads all over the world. He said of not having children, 'You have 'em, I'll entertain 'em.' Thank you so much…

5. Adolf Hitler: enough said, I think.

Dad: I don't think these passport photos do me justice.
Son: You don't want justice, you want mercy.

Diner: Waiter, how long have you worked here?
Waiter: Six months, sir.
Diner: Well it can't have been you who took my order.

Why did the farmer plough his field with a steamroller?
He wanted to grow mashed potatoes.

Son: This loaf is lovely and warm, Mum.
Mum: It should be, the cat's been lying on it all day.

One.

How many mindreaders does it take to change a lightbulb?

What's the difference between a set of traffic lights and a banana?

With traffic lights, green means 'go', yellow means 'slow down' and red means 'stop'.

With a banana, yellow means 'go', green means 'slow down' and red means 'where the hell did you get this banana?!'

Son: I think my teacher likes me.

Dad: Why's that?

Son: She keeps putting kisses all over my work.

Pupil: My budgie died of flu yesterday.

Teacher: Was it bird flu?

Pupil: No, he flew into a car.

Nervous flier: It's my first time in a plane, you will bring me down safely, won't you?

Pilot: I've never left anyone up there yet.

> **What did the green grape say to the purple grape?**
>
> Breathe, you fool, breathe!

Two idiots hired a rowing boat to go fishing and one caught an enormous fish. He got out his pen and put a great big cross on the bottom of the boat.

'That's so we know where to come to catch big fish next time.'

'You idiot! Next time we'll probably get a different boat.'

Dad: Can you get out of the car and tell me if my right indicator's working?

Son: Yes it is … no it isn't … yes it is … no it isn't …

Why didn't the monocles get together?

They didn't want to make a spectacle of themselves.

Two idiots were out for a walk when they came across some tracks. One said they were deer tracks and the other insisted they were fox tracks. They were still arguing when the train hit them.

Teacher: I'm concerned about your son – I asked him who shot Abraham Lincoln and he just said, 'It wasn't me.'
Dad: Well, he might be a bit stupid, but he's honest – if he says it wasn't him, it wasn't him.

What did the buffalo say when her son went to school?
Bi-son.

What do you get when you cross a chicken with a banjo?

A bird that plucks itself.

Why did the hedgehog say 'ouch!'
He'd put his coat on inside out.

Why did the monkey fall out of the tree?
Because he was dead.

> **What goes trot-trot-trot, dash-dash, trot-trot?**
>
> Horse code.

Why did the second monkey fall out of the tree?
He was stuck to the first one.

Why did the third monkey fall out of the tree?
He thought it was a game.

What happened to the two bedbugs who fell in love?
They were married in the spring.

Son: Dad, did you hear they've taken the word 'gullible' out of the latest edition of the dictionary?
Dad: Really?

Son: Did you stand up to Mum like you said you were going to?
Dad: Yes, and she came crawling to me on her hands and knees.
Son: Wow, what did she say?
Dad: 'Come out from under the bed and fight, you coward!'

Son: Mum just said she was a fool when she married you.
Dad: That's true, but I was in love and I didn't notice.

A man walks into a pet shop.
'Have you got any dogs going cheap?' he asks.
'Sorry, all our dogs go woof.'

First man: I have a great new way of saving money. I run home behind the bus and save two pounds every time.
Second man: You ought to run home behind a taxi – then you'd save a tenner.

A policeman was on his rounds when he saw a man walking a crocodile. 'You ought to take that animal to the zoo,' he said.
The next day he saw the same man with the crocodile again.
'I thought I told you to take him to the zoo.'
'I did,' said the man. 'Today I'm taking him to the pictures.'

Two eagles watched a jet fighter zoom past.
'Look at the speed of that.'
'You'd go that fast if your tail was on fire.'

Why don't dogs play poker?
Every time they get a good hand, they wag
their tails.

**Diner: Waiter, this
lobster only has
one claw.**
Waiter: It must have
been in a fight, sir.
**Diner: Well, bring
me the winner.**

**How did the car
get a puncture?**
From the fork in
the road.

Customer: I'd like some nails please.
Assistant: How long do you want them?
Customer: I'd like to keep them.

> Doctor: You're at death's door, but I'm just the man to pull you through.

A ventriloquist walked into a bar.
The man next to him said 'Ouch!'

A man went into a butchers and said, 'I bet you £100 you can't reach that meat on the top shelf without a ladder.'
The butcher thought for a minute and said, 'No bet – the steaks are too high.'

Patient: Doctor, I can't stop singing 'Auld Lang Syne'.
Doctor: I'll have to send you to the Burns unit.

What do you call a man with rubber toes?

Roberto.

A woman was in a Chinese restaurant when a duck came up to her, gave her a bunch of flowers and started serenading to her. She called over the waiter and said, 'You idiot, I ordered aromatic duck!'

Dad: I threw some snow at your mum this morning?
Son: What happened?
Dad: She didn't catch my drift.

Doctor: Say aaah, please.
Patient: Why?
Doctor: My dog died yesterday.

What time does Wimbledon close?

Tennish.

Son: Dad, I ain't got no money.

Dad: How many times do I have to tell you? It's, 'I don't have any money', 'You don't have any money', 'Mum doesn't have any money'…

Son: Blimey, ain't no one in this family got no money?

What happened when the smelliest man in the world bought a pack of Odor-Eaters?
They ate him.

What happened to the cat who ate a ball of wool?
She had mittens.

Why do puffins carry fish in their beaks?
Because they don't have any pockets.

Who has large antlers, big ears and wears white gloves?
Mickey Moose.

What happened to the inside-out goose?
It tickled itself to death.

Why did the unappreciated farmer sit down behind his cow?
He wanted to get a pat on the back.

What's cold and sweet and trundles up the M6 on a stick?
An articulated lolly.

How do you attract a vegetarian?
Make a noise like a wounded lettuce.

What's big, furry and does lots of sit-ups?
The Abdomenable Snowman.

What's nippy, economical and drives round Paris?
The hatchback of Notre Dame.

How does Luke Skywalker get from one place to another?
Ewoks.

What swings through the jungle backwards?
Nazrat.

Burglars broke into the local police station yesterday and stole all the toilets.
The police say they've got nothing to go on.

Why did Harry Potter make his potions in a cauldron?
His microwave was broken.

Why did the actor jump off Nelson's Column?
He wanted to make a big mark in the West End.

What do you call a nervous witch?
A twitch.

Why do witches fly on broomsticks?
They can't get extension leads long enough to fly on vacuum cleaners.

Why is it no good talking to dolphins when they're angry?
You'll just be talking at cross porpoises.

The ants played the elephants at football and just before half-time an elephant trod on the ant centre-forward and squashed him. The elephant was shown a red card.
'But ref,' he said, 'I was only trying to trip him up.'

DAD STAT

13% of Dads hoard anything they get for Father's Day with 'World's Greatest Dad' on it, and bring them out as required over the next 12 months whenever their parenting skills are questioned.

What did the contestant on _I'm a Celebrity_ do when he had to eat either a giant weevil or a normal weevil?

He chose the lesser of two weevils.

How do you make a Venetian blind?

Poke him in the eye.

Why did the unemployed man take a course in meditation?

He said it was better than sitting around all day doing nothing.

What happened at the funeral of the world's worst comedian?
They read out one of his jokes and there was a two-minute silence.

Son: Mum, Dad says he does the work of two men.
Mum: That's right – Laurel and Hardy.

What has two legs, a broom and flies?
The caretaker at a sewage farm.

Diner: Can I have a beefburger without mayonnaise, please?
Waiter: I'm sorry, we've run out of mayonnaise. You can have one without ketchup if you like.

Policeman: I'm investigating the recent spate of burglaries and I'm looking for a man with one eye.
Householder: Why don't you use both eyes, it'll be quicker.

Son: Dad, is it true that every month you hand your pay packet straight over to Mum?
Dad: Yes, son. I just hope she never finds out I get paid weekly.

What happened when the prison van collided with the cement lorry?
Eight hardened criminals escaped.

What happened when the woman Tube driver got married?
She got to the church on time but her train was twenty minutes late.

What's big, green and tastes like cabbage?

The Inedible Hulk.

What happened when the orchestra played a concert in Bermuda?
The man playing the triangle disappeared.

What happened to the man who fell under a steam train?
He was chuffed to bits.

Did you hear how the world's unluckiest man looked in his attic and found an old violin and a painting that turned out to be a Stradivarius and a Rembrandt?
Unfortunately Stradivarius was an awful painter and Rembrandt made terrible violins.

Son: I've got a Saturday job at the bowling alley.
Dad: Ten-pin?
Son: No, it's permanent.

Son: Dad, come and have a water-fight.
Dad: I'll be out in a minute, I'm just boiling the kettle.

What are invisible and smell like bananas?
Monkey farts.

Customer: Do you have a copy of
Psychics Monthly?
Newsagent: You tell me.

Son: Can we play
darts, Dad?
Dad: OK, nearest
to the bull starts.
Son: Mooo!
Dad: Baaaa! You
start then.

How do you make a
Maltese cross?

Tread on his foot.

Son: Dad, there's a man at the door with a
bald head.
Dad: Tell him I've already got one.

Did you hear about the man who went to
a fortune teller because he wanted his
palms read?
She hit them with a hammer.

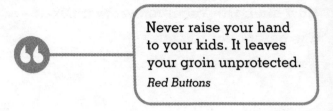

Never raise your hand
to your kids. It leaves
your groin unprotected.
Red Buttons

First footballer: These new boots are killing me.
Second footballer: You should leave them off until
you've got used to them.

**Did you hear what happened when Britain's best
confidence trickster appeared in court?**
He sentenced the judge to three years in prison.

**If there are three budgies in a cage, one on a low
perch, one in the middle and one at the top,
which one owns the cage?**
The one at the bottom, because the other two are
on higher perches.

How did Darth Vader know what Luke Skywalker was getting for Christmas?
Because he had felt his presents.

What does an elephant keep up his trunk?
A six-foot bogey.

A duck walked into a pub wearing a hard hat and carrying a hod.
'A pint of bitter, please,' he said.
'I've never met a talking duck before,' said the barman, 'you ought to get a job in the circus.'
'What would a circus want with a bricklayer?' asked the duck.

Son: Mum, the ladder's fallen down, can you help me put it back up against the wall?
Mum: I'm busy, tell your dad.
Son: He already knows, he's hanging from the guttering.

What did the ocean say to the shore?
Nothing, it just waved.

A man jumped into a taxi and said, 'Prince Edward's Close'.
'Don't worry,' said the driver, 'we'll lose him at the next traffic lights.'

Patient: What's wrong with me, doctor? I wake up in the morning, look in the mirror and feel sick.
Doctor: Well, there's nothing wrong with your eyesight.

Did you hear about the idiot who worked in a china factory?
He locked himself in the kiln one night so they fired him.

> **How do you turn a cat into a dog?**
>
> Throw it on the fire and it'll go wooooof!

How do you get rid of an actor when he calls at your house?
Pay him for the pizza.

First guest: This is supposed to be a fancy-dress party but you've just come carrying a girl on your back.
Second guest: I've come as a snail.
First guest: And the girl?
Second guest: That's Michelle.

How do you catch a unique rabbit?
U-nique up on him.

How do you catch a tame rabbit?
The tame way, u-nique up on him.

Son: I got sent out of maths today. The teacher asked me what 3 times 4 was and I said 12, but then she asked me what 4 times 3 was.
Dad: You idiot, they're the same!
Son: That's exactly what I said to her.

Did you hear about the man who bought a bottle of HP sauce?
He had to pay 5p a week for two years.

Diner: Could you call me a taxi, please.
Waiter: Certainly, sir. You're a taxi.

Surgeon: Now just relax, there's no need to worry.

Patient: But it's my first operation and I'm really nervous.

Surgeon: Well, it's my first operation and I'm not nervous at all.

Doctor: Do you want the good news or the bad news?

Patient: The good news.

Doctor: You're going to have a disease named after you.

Why do hens lay eggs?
If they dropped them they'd break.

How do you get Pikachu on to a bus?

Poke him on.

Why did the nose cross the road?
He was tired of getting picked on.

Policeman: I think you should be wearing glasses when you're driving.
Motorist: But I have contacts.
Policeman: I don't care who you know, I'm still giving you a ticket.

What does a meerkat put on his fingers while he's sewing?
Thimbles!

Why do gorillas have big nostrils?
Because they have big fingers.

Son: Dad, why don't we go and live in Jeopardy?
Dad: Where's that?
Son: I don't know, but I heard on the news there were hundreds of jobs there.

An idiot was at a vending machined shovelling more and more money in as can after can of Coke came out.

'When are you going to be finished?' asked the man behind him.

'Buzz off,' said the idiot, 'can't you see I'm winning?'

Son: Dad, when are you going to report your stolen credit card?

Dad: I don't think I'll bother. The thief is spending less than your mum did.

Why does a surgeon wear a mask when he's operating?

So the patient won't recognise him if he kills them.

Why did the elephants all wear red shirts?

They were on the same team.

How do you make a sculpture of an elephant?
Get a big lump of rock and chip away all the bits
that don't look like an elephant.

**Never criticise someone until you've walked a
mile in their shoes.**
Then, when you criticise them, they're a mile away
and you've got their shoes.

**How many Spaniards does it take to change
a lightbulb?**
Juan.

**The cook was putting the ingredients into her
massive cooking pot.**
'Have some carrots, Ronald ... have some potatoes,
Ronald ... have some onions, Ronald.'
**'Why are you talking to your pot like that,' asked
her friend.**
'Because it's called Ron.'

Which horse is better at karaoke, one with big hooves or one with little hooves?
The one with little hooves, because the one with big hooves is the shyer horse.

How sharp are butchers' knives?

Butcher finger on that block and you'll find out.

Did you hear about the idiot who ran the marathon?
He was so tired after 20 miles he had to turn round and go back to the start.

Who are the nuttiest officers in the army?

The kernels.

What do you call a man with a prison on his head?
Nick.

What do you call a man with an oil rig on his head?
Derek.

Two men met 500 feet up in the air.
The one coming down said, 'Do you know anything about parachutes?'
The one going up said, 'No, do you know anything about gas cookers?'

Teacher: You were supposed to draw a picture from the Bible – what's that aeroplane doing there?
Pupil: It's the Flight from Egypt, and that's Pontius the Pilot.

Rambler: Why has that pig got a wooden leg?
Farmer: That's a very special pig. It's got 10 O levels, 4 A levels, a first-class degree, a PhD and a Nobel Prize … when you find a pig like that, you don't eat it all at once.

A Christian was in the arena when the lion was released. The lion came right up to him, knelt down and started praying.
'It's a miracle!' said the Christian.
'Actually,' said the lion, 'I'm just saying grace.'

Applicant: What hours would I have to work?
Shopkeeper: All hours, we're a convenience store.
Applicant: That doesn't sound very convenient to me.

How do you cut down a tree with a bicycle?

Use a chopper.

Doctor: I'm afraid you only have a month to live.
Patient: What should I do?
Doctor: Well, don't start watching any serials.

Doctor: I'm afraid you only have four minutes to live.
Patient: Can't you do anything for me?
Doctor: I could boil you an egg.

Conductor: When someone can't play any instruments they give them two sticks and sit them by the drums.
Drummer: And if they can't even cope with that they take one of the sticks away and make them stand at the front.

Is Karl Marx really buried in Highgate Cemetery?
Or is it just a Communist plot?

Why are you stuffing those fried rook pieces into your computer?
They're my crow chips.

Patient: Doctor, my mouth feels all prickly and smelly.
Doctor: Ah, you must have hollytosis.

Why did the decorator nail a rug to the wall?
He wanted to give it a mat finish.

What did the grocer say when he ran out of onions?
That's shallot.

Dad: I wrote the car off today when I dipped the headlights.
Mum: How on earth can dipping the headlights write off the car?
Dad: I drove into the canal.

How did the mailman break his foot when he dropped the post on it?

It was a concrete post.

Did you hear about the idiot who was on the escalator when it broke down?

He was stuck there for three hours.

What did the dyslexic, agnostic insomniac do?

Lay awake all night wondering whether there was a dog.

What's white, unique and goes up?

A confused snowflake.

What pop group do you get when you cross A Christmas Carol with Moby Dick?

Jacob Marley and the Whalers.

Son: Dad, can you help with my science homework? What's a brain cell for?
Dad: Well, yours would be quite expensive because it's never been used.

Why did the homeless genie run away from fights?
He'd lost his bottle.

What do you use to wrap an orange?

Jaffa tape.

What do you say to a pair of sore lips?
Hello, chaps.

What's the quickest way to get through check-in at an airport?
Just trip over your luggage and go flying.

Two crows were talking about their families.
One said to the other, 'Bred any good rooks lately?'

Did you hear about the man who was given a job and sacked the same day?
He was dis-appointed.

What's Robin Hood's favourite radio programme?
The Archers.

Patient: Doctor, whatever I come to see you with, you just send me to the gym, why?
Doctor: Because gym'll fix it.

Who was the
first Irish
President of
the United
States?
Barack O'Bama.

Salesman: We fitted your double-glazing two years ago and you still haven't paid for it.
Idiot: I didn't know I had to – you told me that after 12 months it would pay for itself.

Why did the stupid forger get caught?
He tried to use too many of his seven-pound notes at once.

Son: Dad, there's a superhero in the bath, and I think it's Spiderman.
Dad: What makes you think it's Spiderman?
Son: He can't get out.

Dad: I took your old Cluedo to the charity shop today, but I told them it was always Colonel Mustard who did it.
Son: Why did you have to give the game away?

What do you call a hundred labourers falling down a hill?
A navvylanche.

What's red and stupid?
A blood clot.

DIY assistant: What do you want, you moron?
Customer: If you're going to talk to me like that, I'm having all those wooden panels and posts.
Assistant: I'm sorry, please don't take a fence.

It must be great to be able to use your left hand as well as your right. I'd give my right arm to be ambidextrous.

A blind man went into a shop, picked up his guide dog and started swinging it round his head.
'Can I help you, sir?' asked a nervous assistant.
'No, thanks, I'm just looking round.'

What did the vicar say when he was served a piece of dodgy fish?
This must be the piece of cod that passeth understanding.

Customer: Have you got anything by The Doors?
Record-shop assistant: Just a fire extinguisher.

What's the longest word in the dictionary?
'Smiles' – there's a mile between the first and last letter.

How do toads see in the mist?

With frog lamps.

What's the difference between a dead fox in the road and a dead banker?

There are skid marks before the fox.

First chairman: Buying this football club made me a millionaire.

Second chairman: What were you before you bought it?

First chairman: A multimillionaire.

Executioner: Before I throw the switch, do you have a last request?

Prisoner: I'm a bit nervous, would you hold my hand?

What exactly is a mermaid?

A deep she-fish.

Do you know what you get if you cross alphabet soup with a bomb?

No, but if it goes off it could spell disaster.

First boy: My dad's just bought some horse manure to put on his rhubarb.
Second boy: Oh, we usually have custard on ours.

Why were the elephants the last to leave the ark?
Because they had to pack their trunks.

What's hairy, scary and has a pair a knickers of its head?
An underwear wolf.

What do you call a bogey in a crash helmet?
A snail.

How many Dads does it take to wallpaper a room?
Three if you slice them thinly.

Policeman: I want you to go straight home:
Man: I can't.
Policeman: Why not?
Man: Because I live round the corner.

What fairground ride is always made of iron?
A ferrous wheel.

Teacher: Can you tell me what language is spoken on Corsica.
Pupil: Course I can.

What happened to the decorater when his mate dropped a tin of paint on his head?
He was overcome with emulsion.

Auntie: Have some sweets, Jimmy.
Jimmy: I'll just have one, Auntie, thank you.
Auntie: Oh, you don't need to be so polite.
Jimmy: All right, I'll just have one, you mad old bat.

Patient: Doctor, I'm allergic to lapels.
Doctor: Ah, you've got cholera.

What type of car did the cowboy drive?
An 'owdy.

Why don't little children have their pockets picked?
No one would stoop that low.

Mechanic: There's good news and bad news; the bad news is I couldn't mend your brakes.
Motorist: What's the good news?
Mechanic: I found a way to turn the volume up on your horn.

Doctor: I'm afraid you've got Heathrow disease.
Patient: Can you cure me?
Doctor: No, it's terminal.

Why did the boy take a ruler to bed?

He wanted to see how long he slept.

Policeman: I'd like you to blow in this bag, sir.

Motorist: But I haven't been drinking!

Policeman: I know, but my chips are too hot.

Customer: Three pounds of potatoes, please.

Grocer: Sorry, we only sell kilos now.

Customer: Oh right, well, three pounds of kilos then.

Why did the idiot get a job as a postman?

He thought it would be better than walking the streets.

What do you need to know to be an auctioneer?

Lots.

What does James Bond eat at Christmas?

Mince Spies.

Why couldn't the idiot get out of the hotel?
He was OK with the doors marked 'push' and 'pull', but then he reached one that said 'lift'.

Why did the boy go to his exam with a pair of trainers on his head?
He wanted to jog his memory.

What happened to the Dutch woman with inflatable shoes?
She popped her clogs.

A hyena and an elephant were walking through the jungle when the hyena was attacked by a lion. After a ferocious struggle the hyena managed to get away.
'Why didn't you help?' he asked the elephant.
'You were laughing so much I thought you were enjoying it ...'

Surprisingly, 84% of Dads eat more fruit and veg than their kids – however, this figure falls to 23% when you exclude Dads who include as fruit and veg: 1) potatoes 2) fruit pastilles 3) real ale

Son: Dad, can Gran come down for the weekend?
Dad: Why?
Son: Well, she's been up on the roof for a month now.

Doctor: I think you're suffering from hypochondria.
Patient: Not that as well?

Where do sick farm animals go to get better?
To the horsepital in a hambulance.

How easy is it to please a fat person?
A piece of cake.

216

An Englishman was in a restaurant in Paris when he found a fly in his soup and decided to show off his basic French.

'Voici le mouche,' he said to the waiter.

The waiter inspected the soup and said, 'La mouche, monsieur.'

'If you say so, but you must have better eyesight than I have.'

A boy was looking through an old family photo album.

Boy: Who's that man in the swimming trunks?

Mum: Your dad.

Boy: Then who's the fat old bald bloke that lives with us now?

Son: Dad, can you lend me ten pounds?

Dad: Yes, but remember, a fool and his money are soon parted.

Son: Yes, I just worked that out.

> **Why did the receipt cross the road?**
>
> It was stapled to the chicken.

Man: I want you to have a look at my cat.

Vet: Is it a tom?

Man: No, I've brought it with me.

Why did the idiot wake up in the morning to find a plane outside his bedroom?

He'd left the landing light on.

Why did the Eskimo do his washing in Tide?

Because it was too cold out tide.

Why was the pie standing on the corner of the street?

He was meetin' potato.

> **What do you call a man with a truck on his head?**
>
> Lawrie.

What's acoustic?
It's what a Scottish
farmer uses to
control his cattle.

**How did Bob
Marley like his
doughnuts?**

With jam in.

What's a wombat?
Something you play wom with.

**Mum: Since it started snowing all Jimmy's done is
look through the window.**
Dad: Well, if it gets any worse you can let him in.

**Son: Why did you buy this TV? It's stuck on
full volume.**
Dad: I know, but it was so cheap I couldn't turn
it down.

Do you know how long cows should be milked?
The same way as short cows.

What do you call a judge with no thumbs?
Justice Fingers.

What was the Scottish cloakroom attendant called?
Angus McCoatup.

What was the Indian cloakroom attendant called?
Mahatma Coat.

What should you do if see a spaceman?
Park in it, dude!

What sort of shoes does Winnie the Pooh wear?
None, he has bear feet.

What do you call a well-behaved badger?
A goodger.

What's the difference between a kangeroo and a kangeroot?
One is an Australian mammal and the other is a Geordie stuck in a lift.

Woman: Can I have some sleeping pills for my husband, please?
Doctor: What's the matter with him?
Woman: He keeps waking up.

What do you do if you've lost a vicar?
Contact missing parsons.

What was Beethoven's fifth favourite fruit?
Ba-na-na-na!

Why couldn't Dracula's wife get to sleep?
Because of his coffin.

Why didn't the quarter jump off the building with the nickel?
Because it had more cents.

Teacher: What does 'coincidence' mean?
Pupil: That's funny, I was just going to ask you that.

What's the difference between ammonia and pneumonia?
Ammonia comes in bottles and pneumonia comes in chests.

What fur do you get from a lion?
As fur as possible.

Pupil: Can you still live when your brain stops working?
Teacher: You're alive, aren't you?

Why is gravity useful?
When you drop something it's much easier to pick it off the floor than the ceiling.

Did you hear about the boy who put a clean pair of socks on every day?
By the end of the week he couldn't get his shoes on.

Why did the poet have to find a proper job?
He realised that rhyme doesn't pay.

What did the two snails do when they had a fight?

They slugged it out.

Portico publishes a range of books that
are fresh, funny and forthright.

PORTICO

An imprint of **Pavilion** Books